Mama, Who Lives in the Forest

Cheryl L Jordan

For permission contact www.withcheryllee.ca

ISBN Paperback: 978-1-7781235-0-4
ISBN Hardcover: 978-1-7781235-9-7

Wagging Tales
Publishing

Dedicated to my loving wife for supporting
my dreams in writing a children's book.

Mama, who lives in the forest?

A squirrel lives in the forest
with her kit.

Mama, who lives in the forest?

A snake lives in the forest
with her snakelets.

Mama, who lives in the forest?

A raccoon lives in the forest
with her cubs.

Mama, who lives in the forest?

A frog lives in the forest
with her froglet.

Mama, who lives in the forest?

A bear lives in the forest with her cub.

Mama, who lives in the forest?

An owl lives in the forest
with her owlettes.

Mama, who lives in the forest?

A deer lives in the forest
with her fawns.

Mama, who lives in the forest?

A fox lives in the forest
with her pup.

Mama, who lives in the forest?

A skunk lives in the forest with her kits.

Mama, who lives in the forest?

A mouse lives in the forest
with her pups.

Mama,
who lives in the forest?

An eagle lives in the forest with her eaglets.

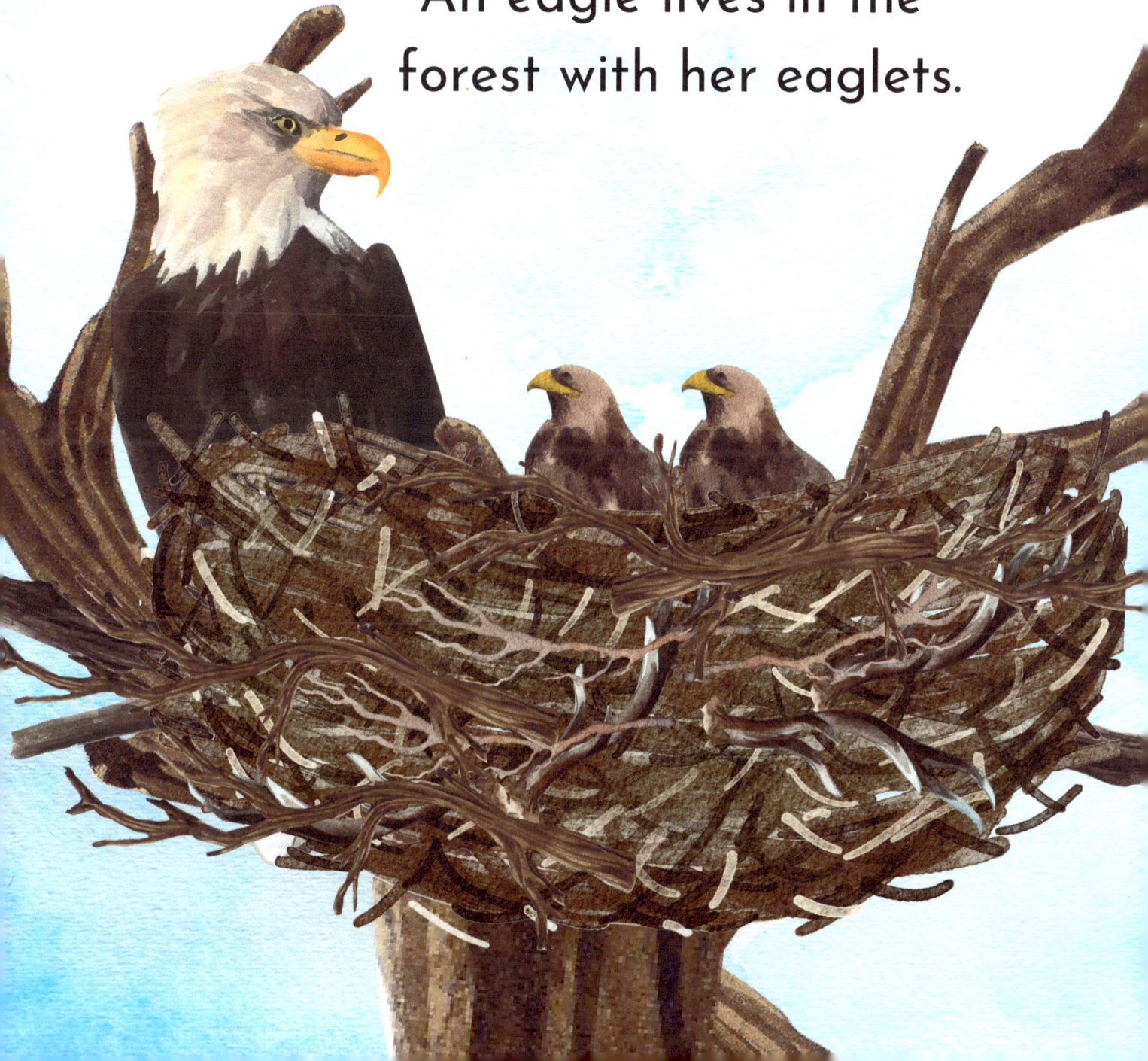

Mama, who lives in the forest?

A lizard lives in the forest
with her hatchling.

Mama, tell me again,
who lives in the forest?

My little kit,
we all live in the forest.

Parents, please note that some baby animals have more than one name. In this story, we've used common names to keep things simple and enjoyable for young readers.

Aslo in the Little Rabbit Series

Little Rabbit
Discovers Spring

written by
Cheryl L Jordan

For other children's books and activity books, visit
www.withcheryllee.ca

www.ingramcontent.com/pod-product-compliance
Lightning Source LLC
Chambersburg PA
CBHW042107040426
42448CB00002B/170